I0462455

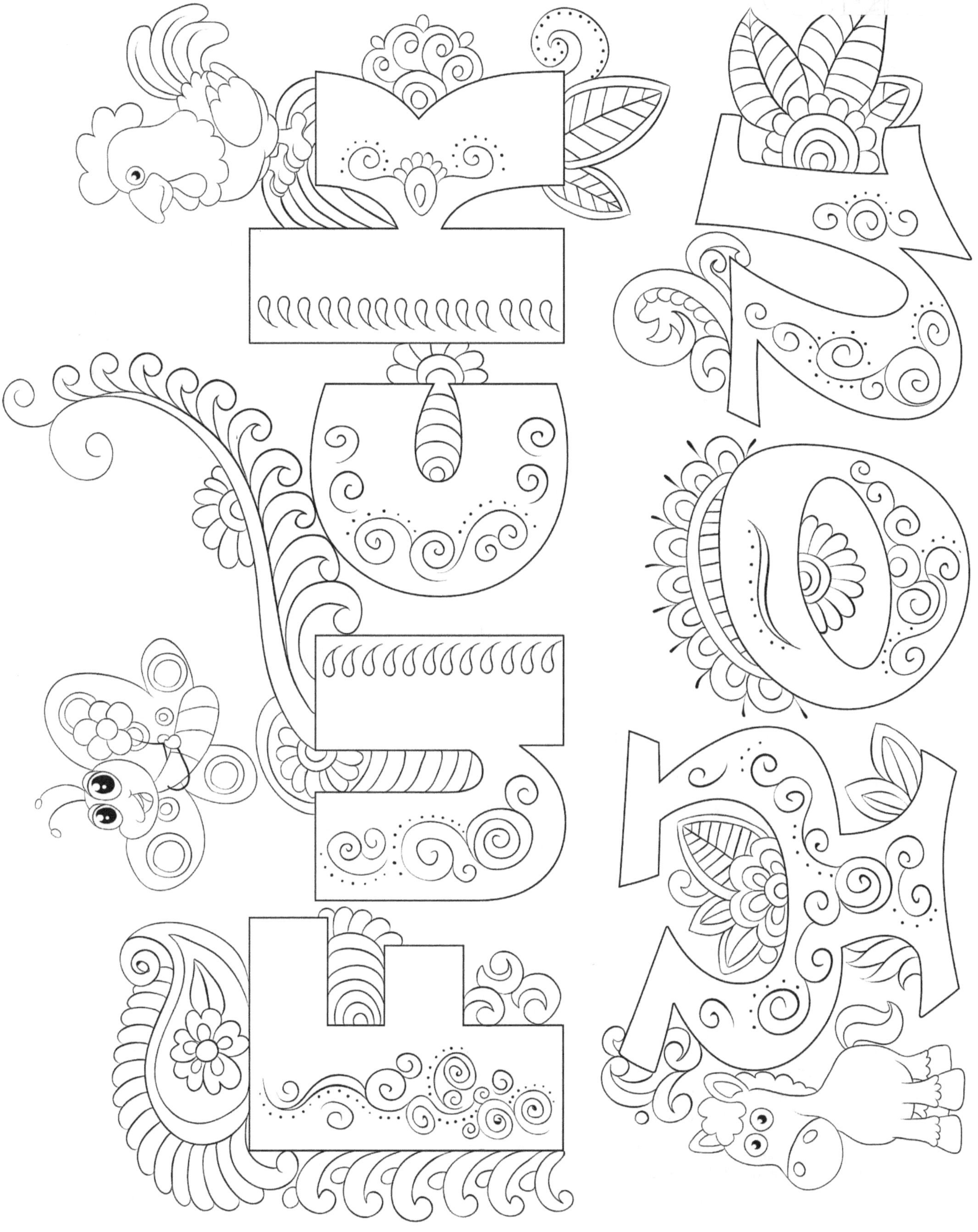

ISBN: 978-1523906147

Illustrated by:
Mandala & Caricature Illustration
Joshua Lazana Lagman and Jade Villaremo

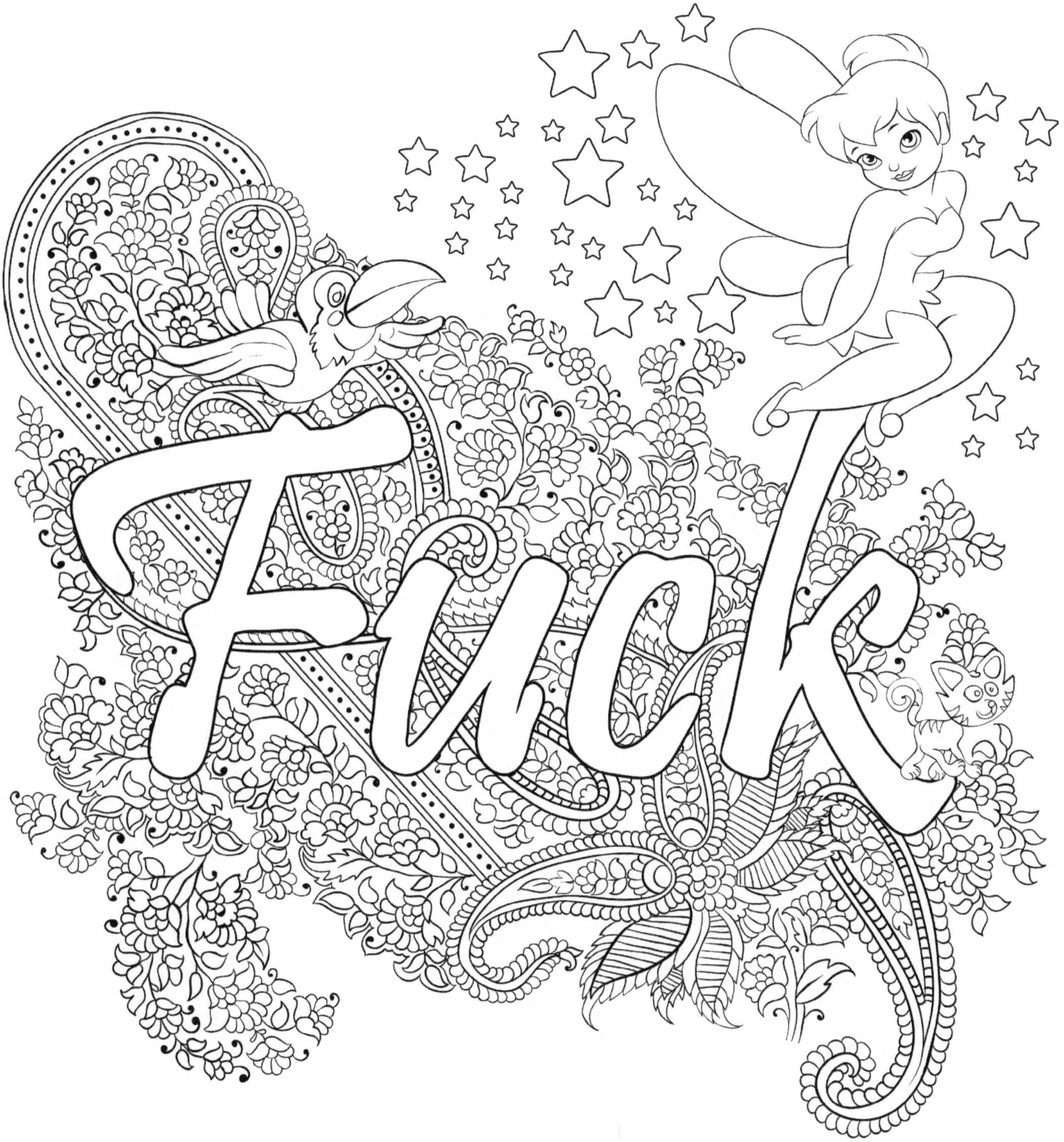
Fuck

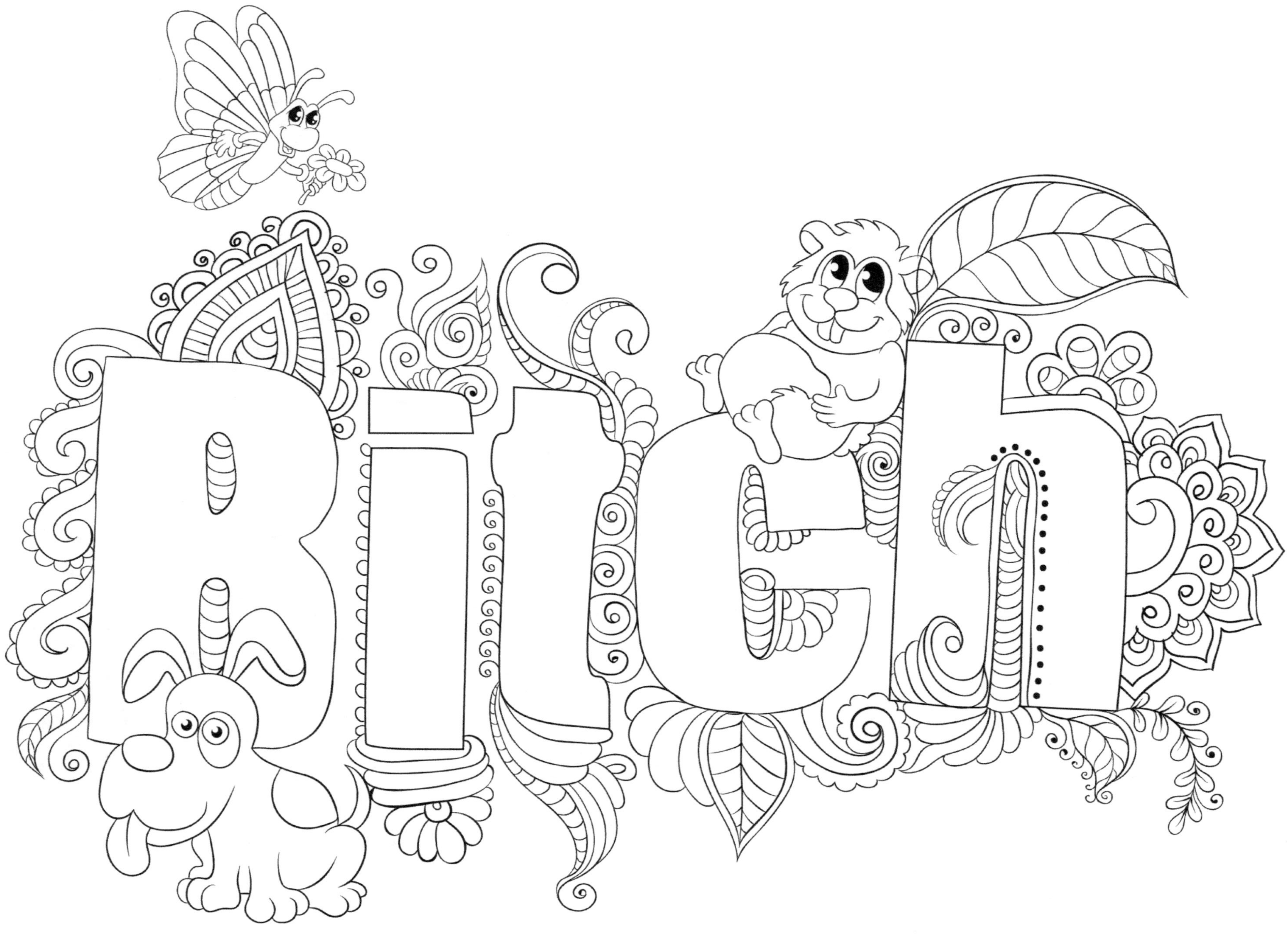
Bitch

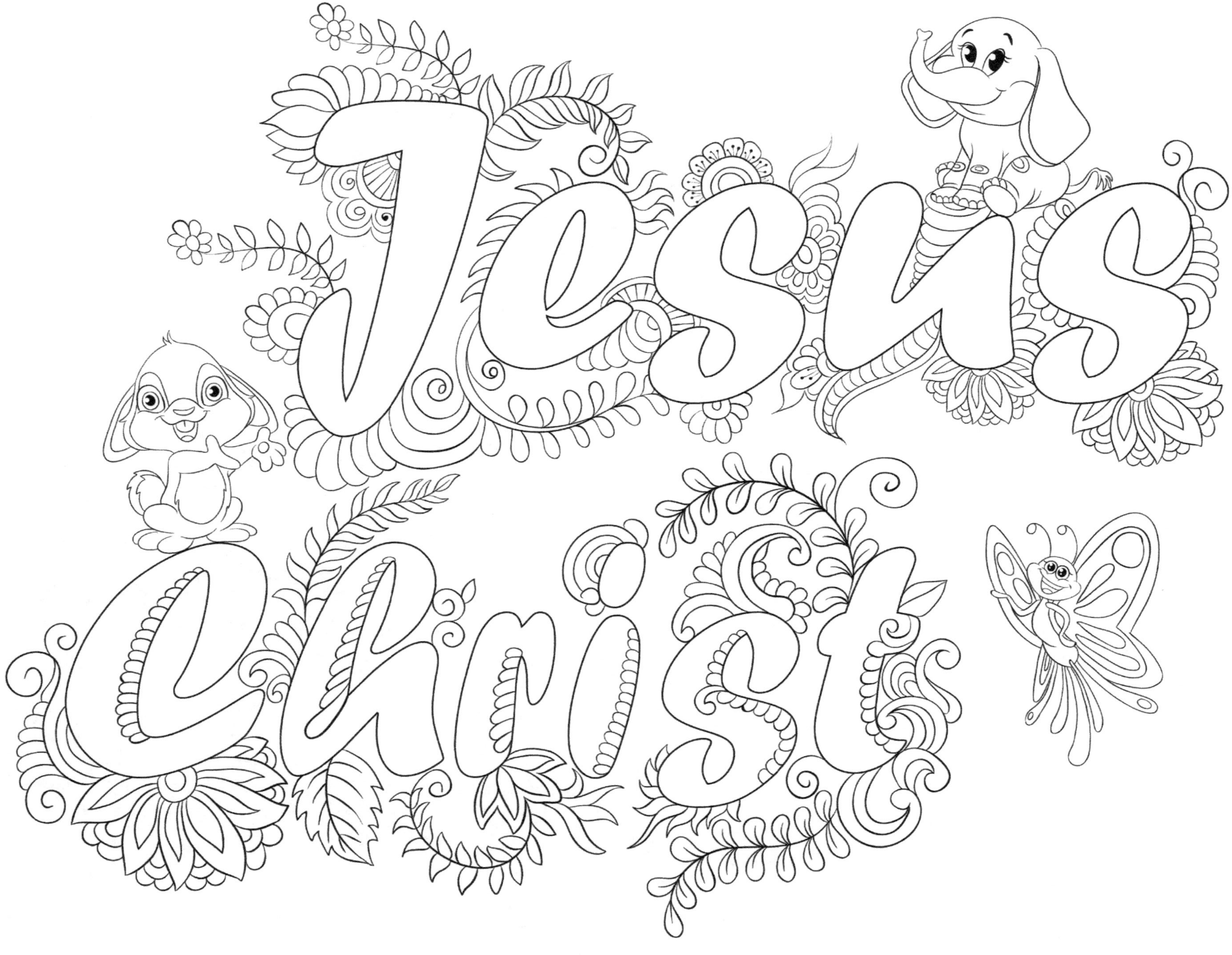
Jesus
Christ

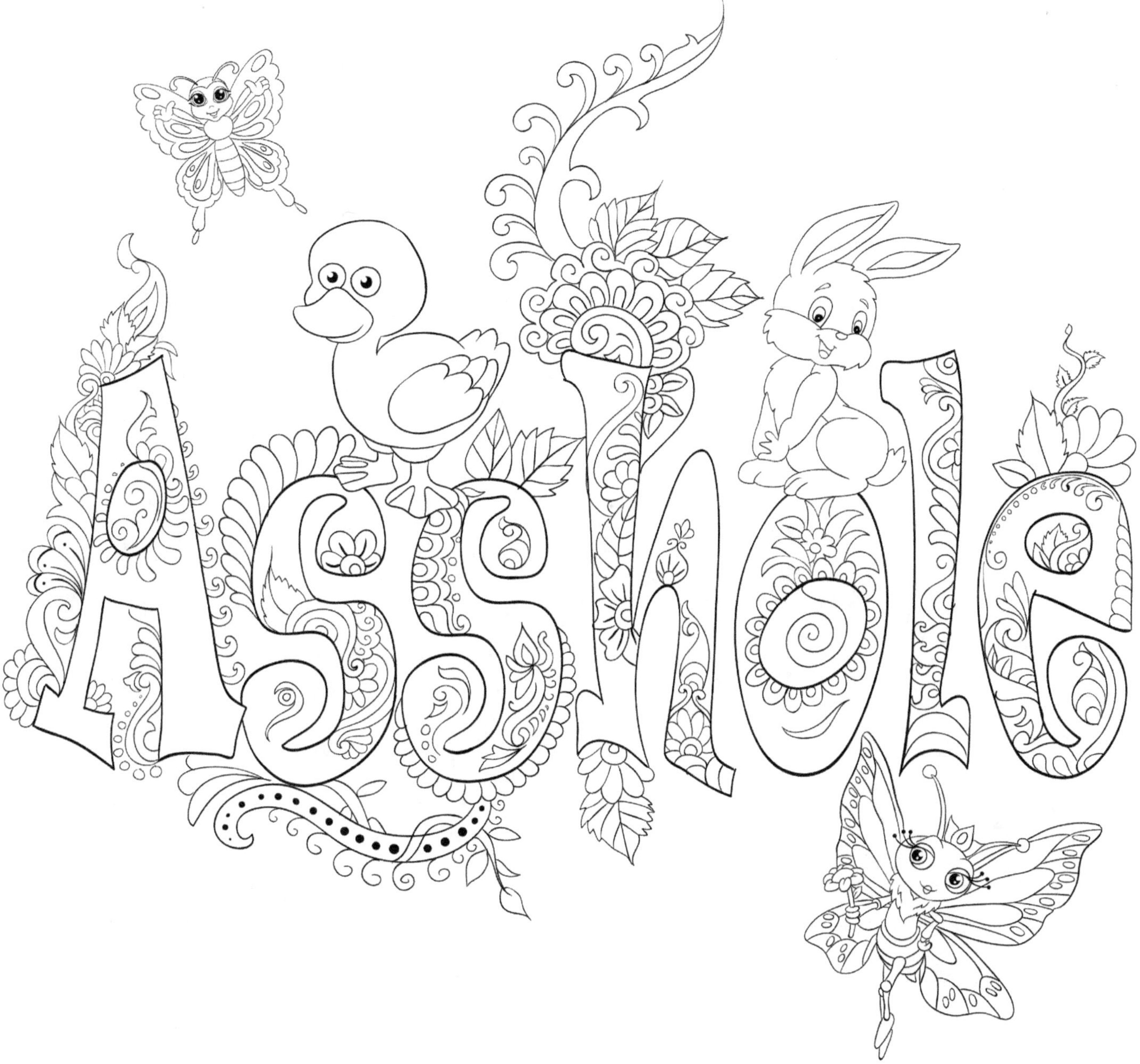
Asshole

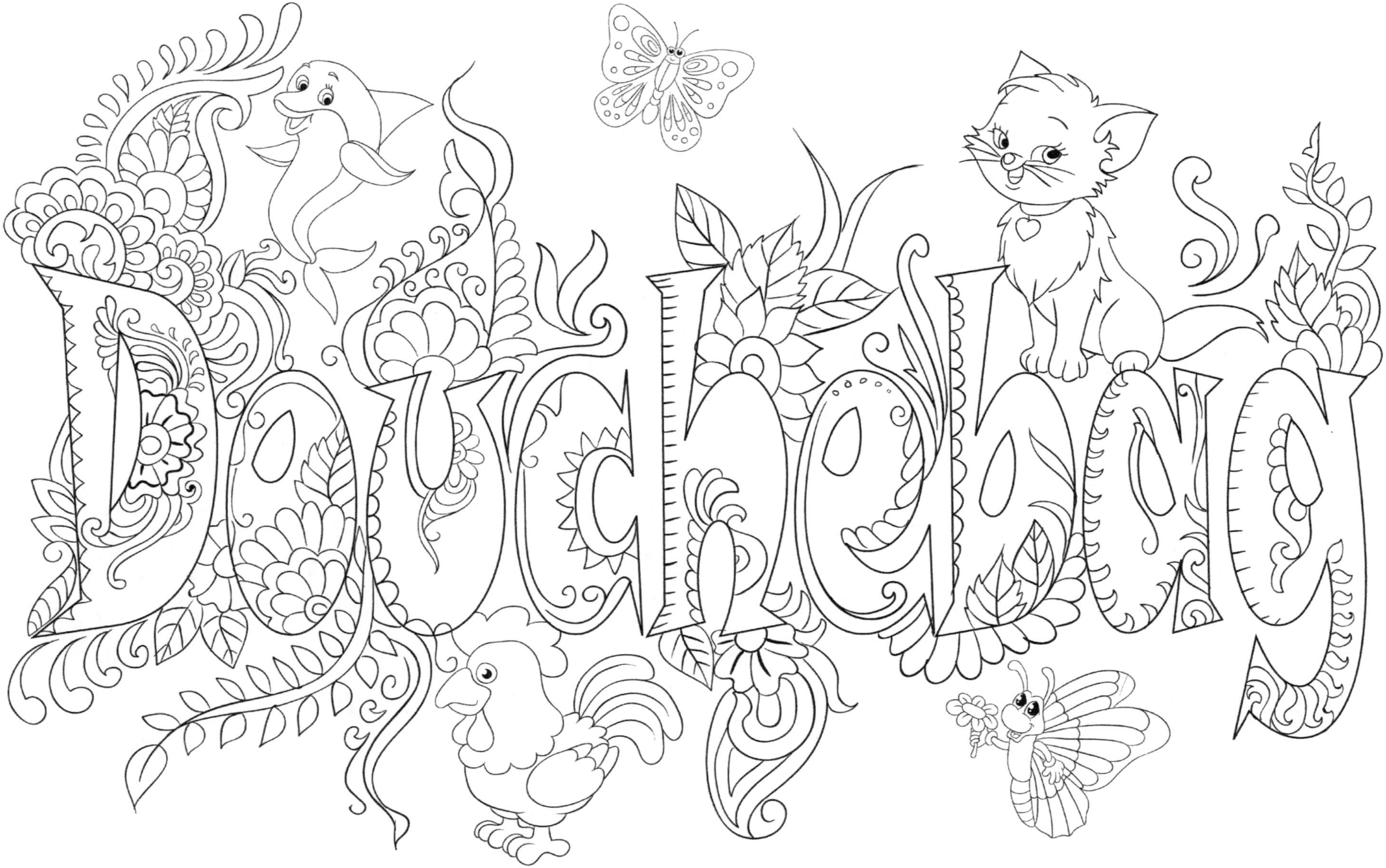
Douchebag

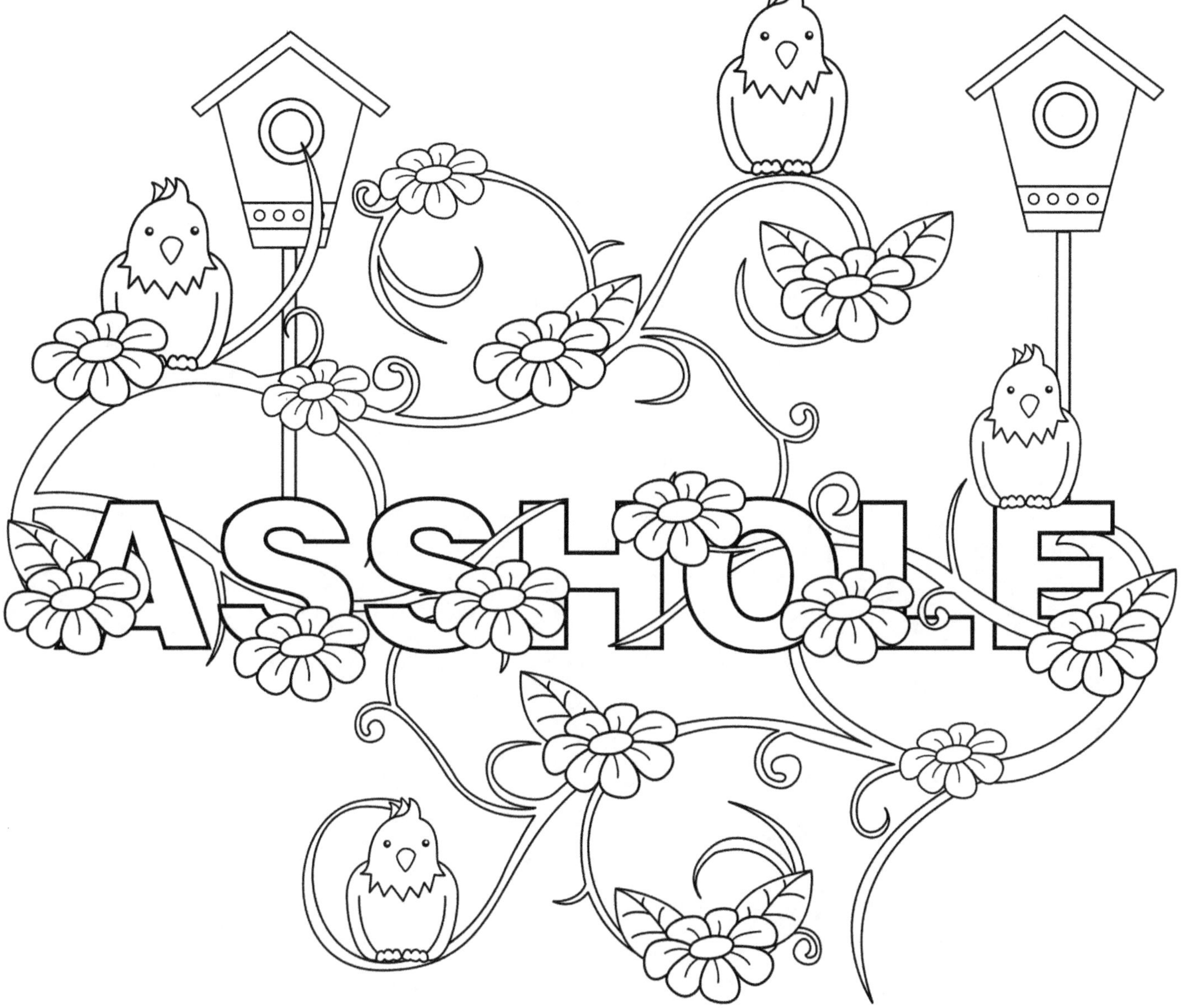
ASSHOLE

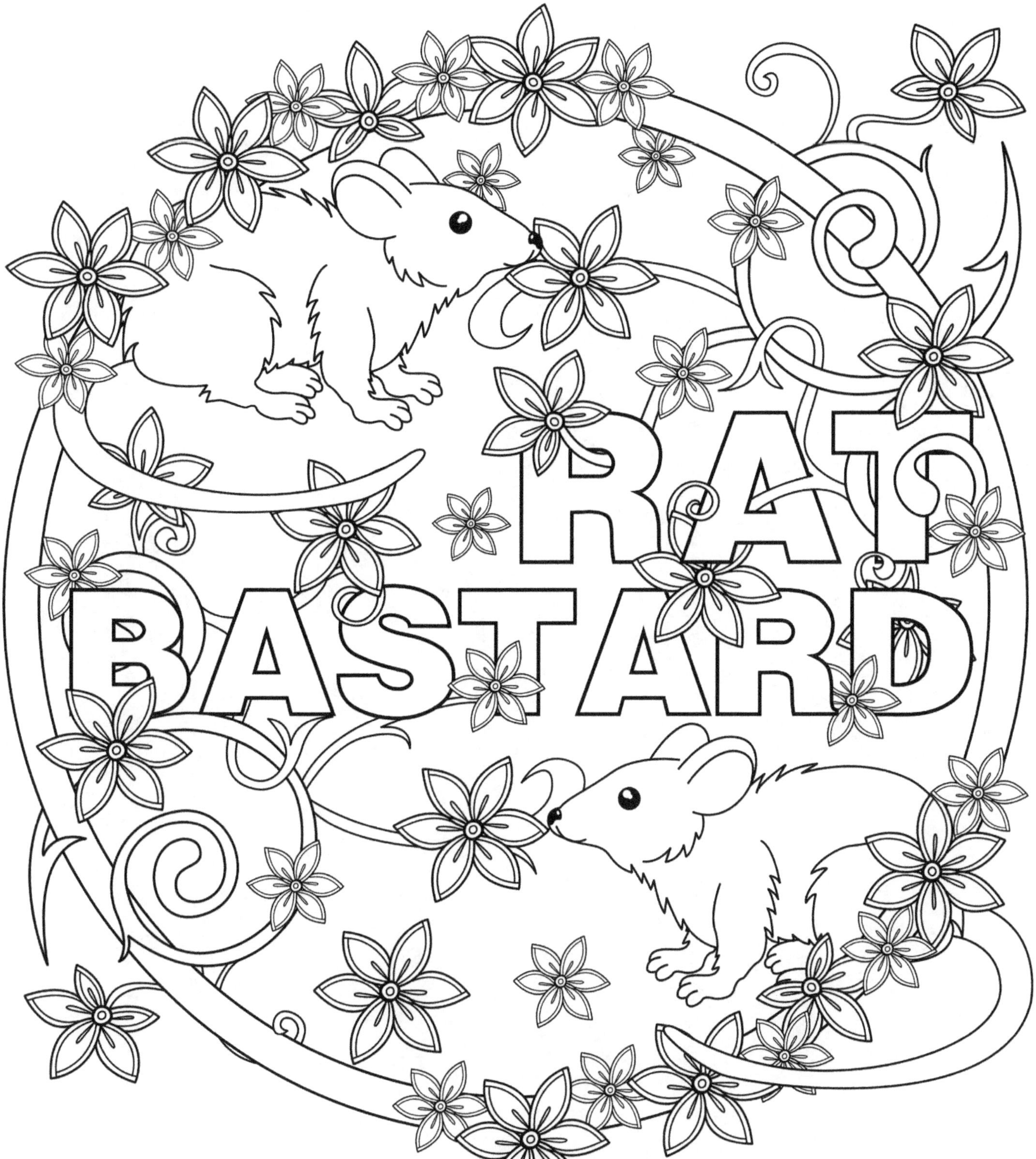
RAT
BASTARD

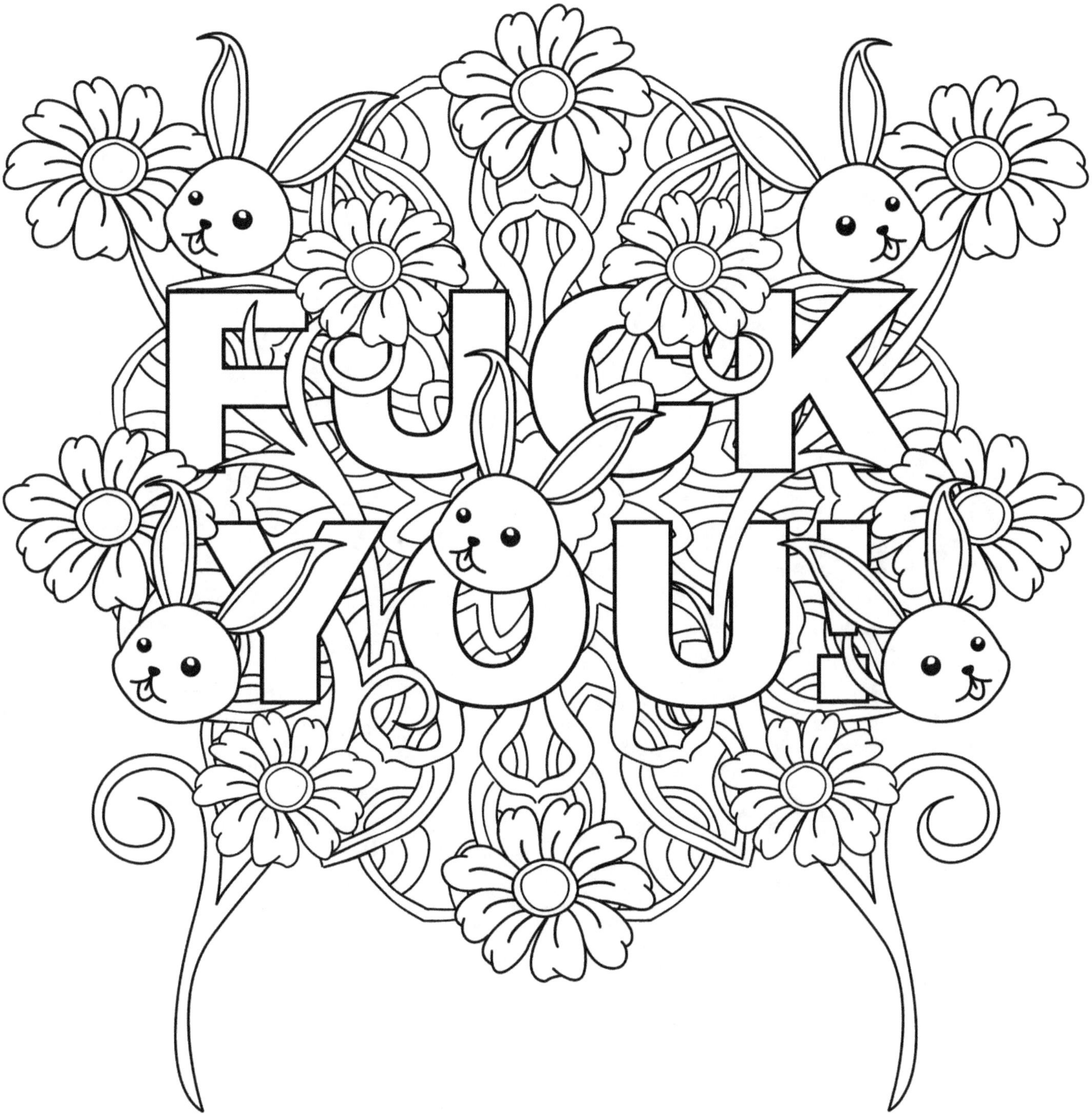
FUCK
YOU!

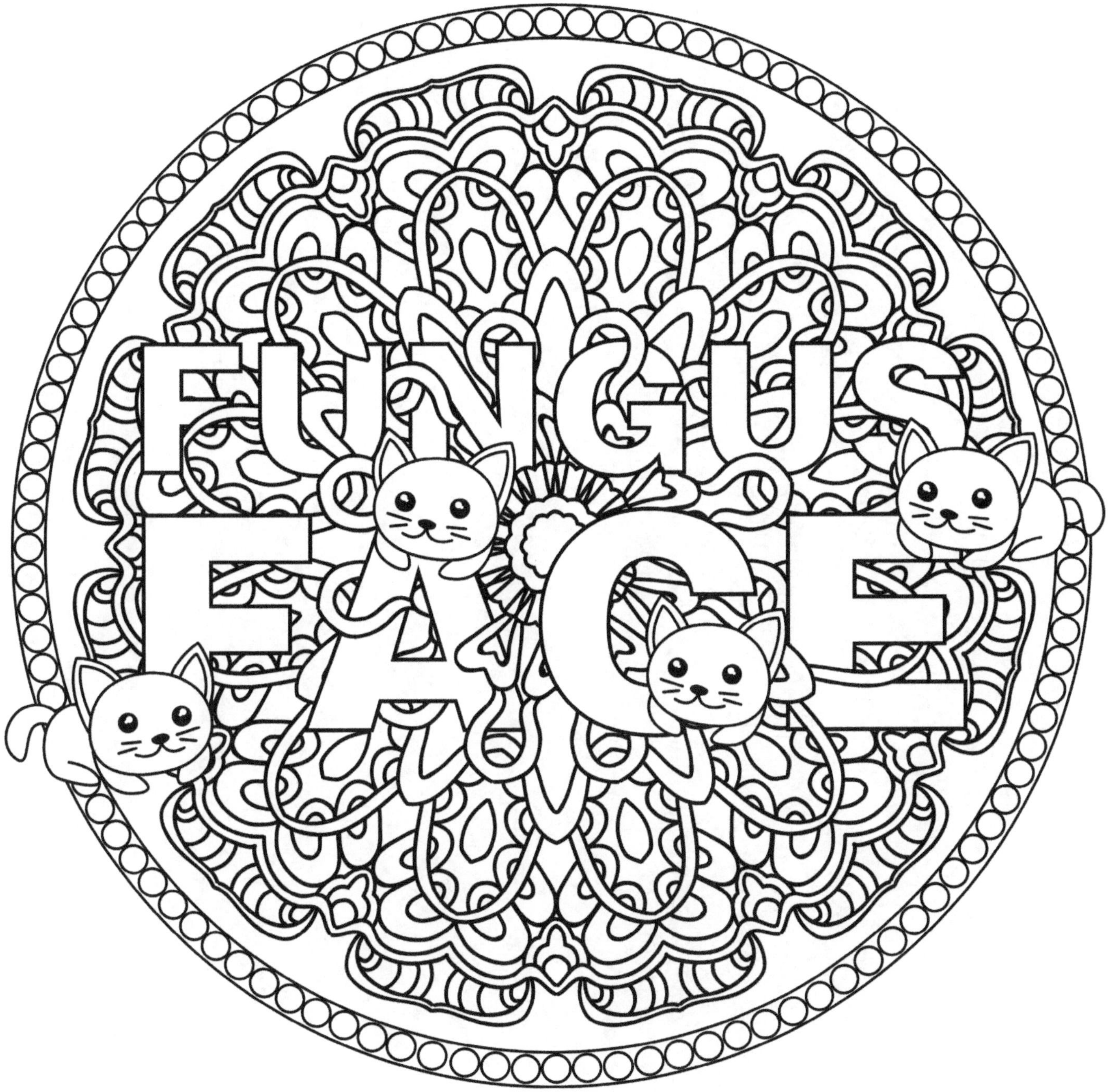
FUNGUS
FACE

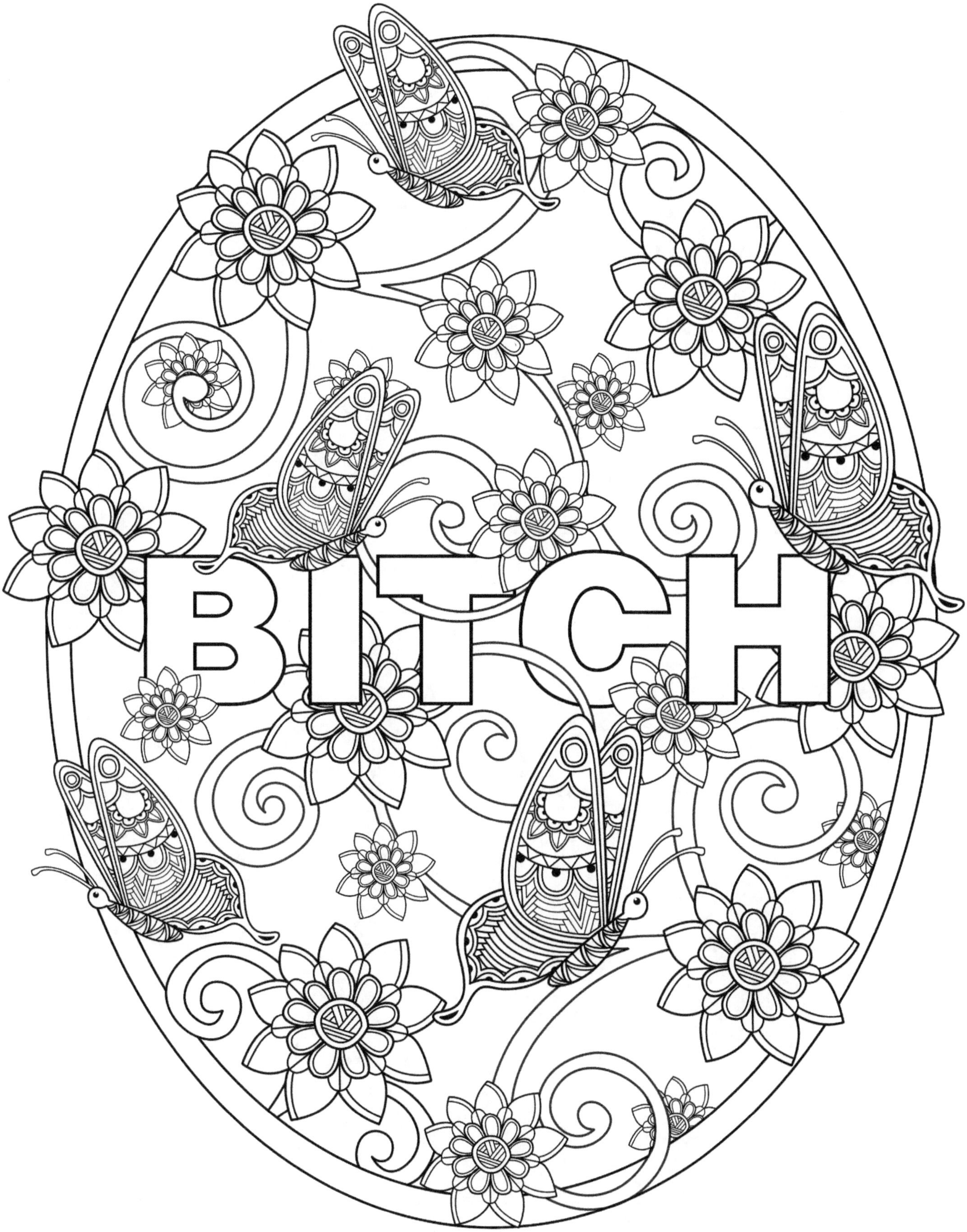
BITCH

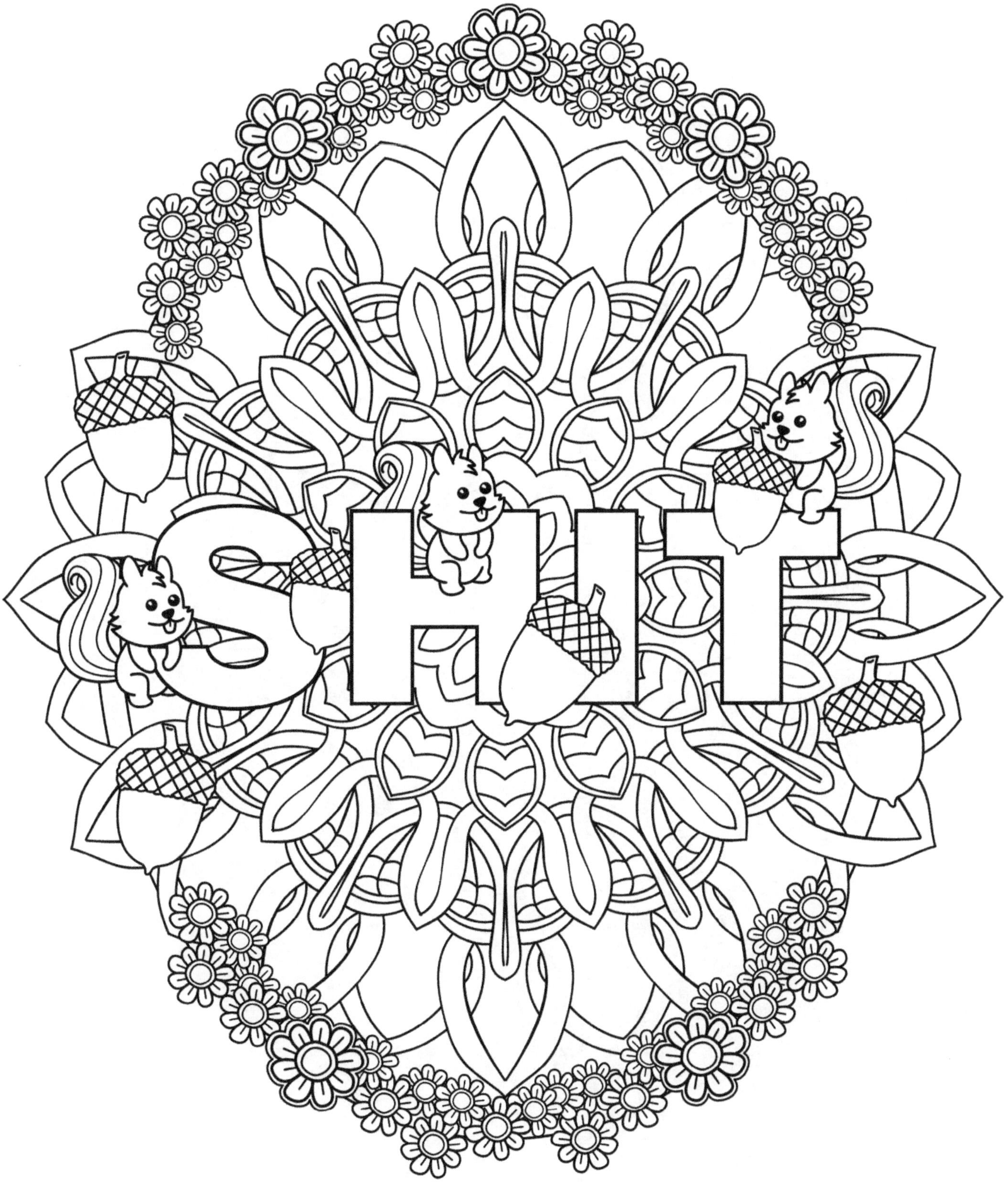
SHIT

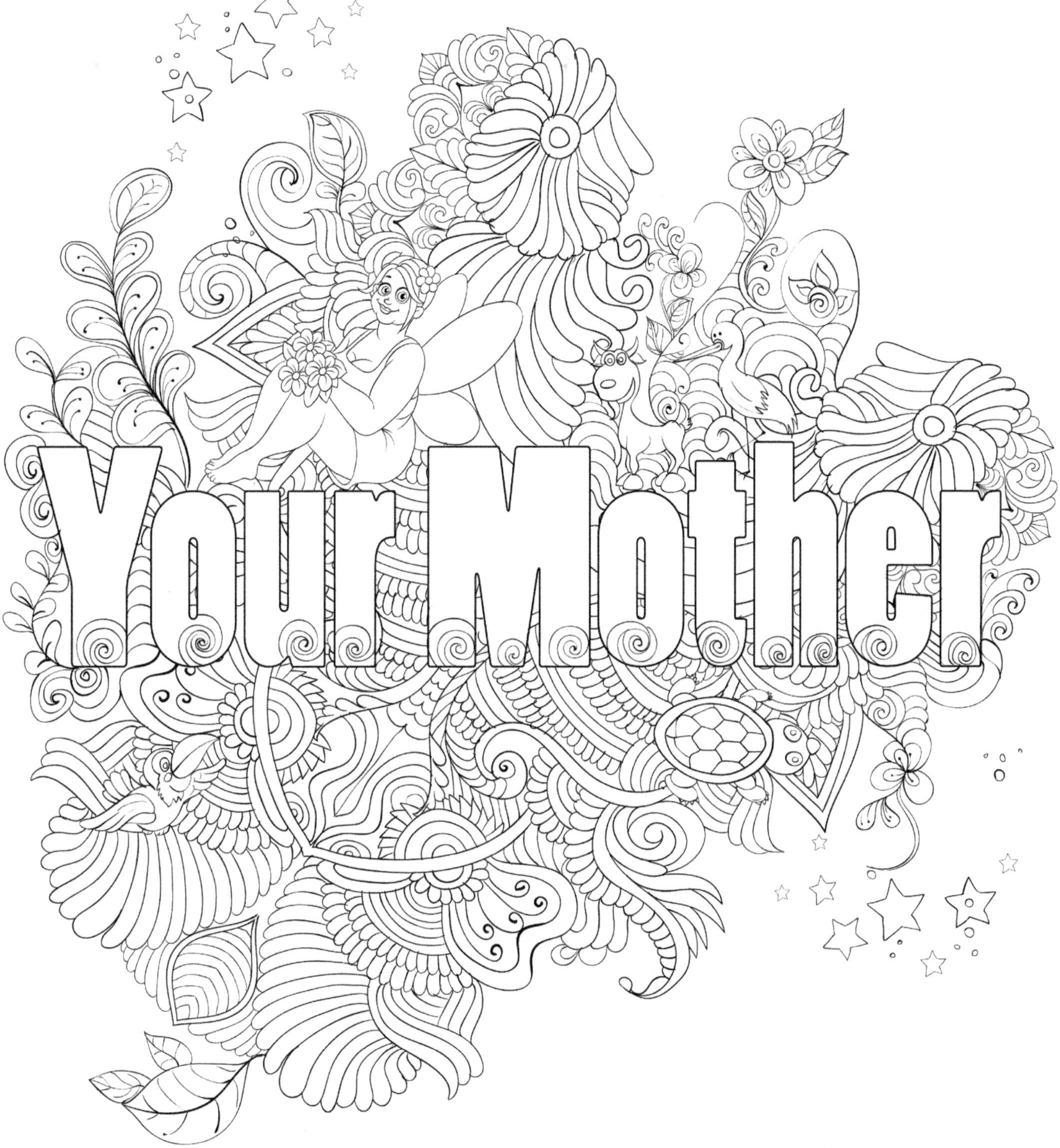
Your Mother

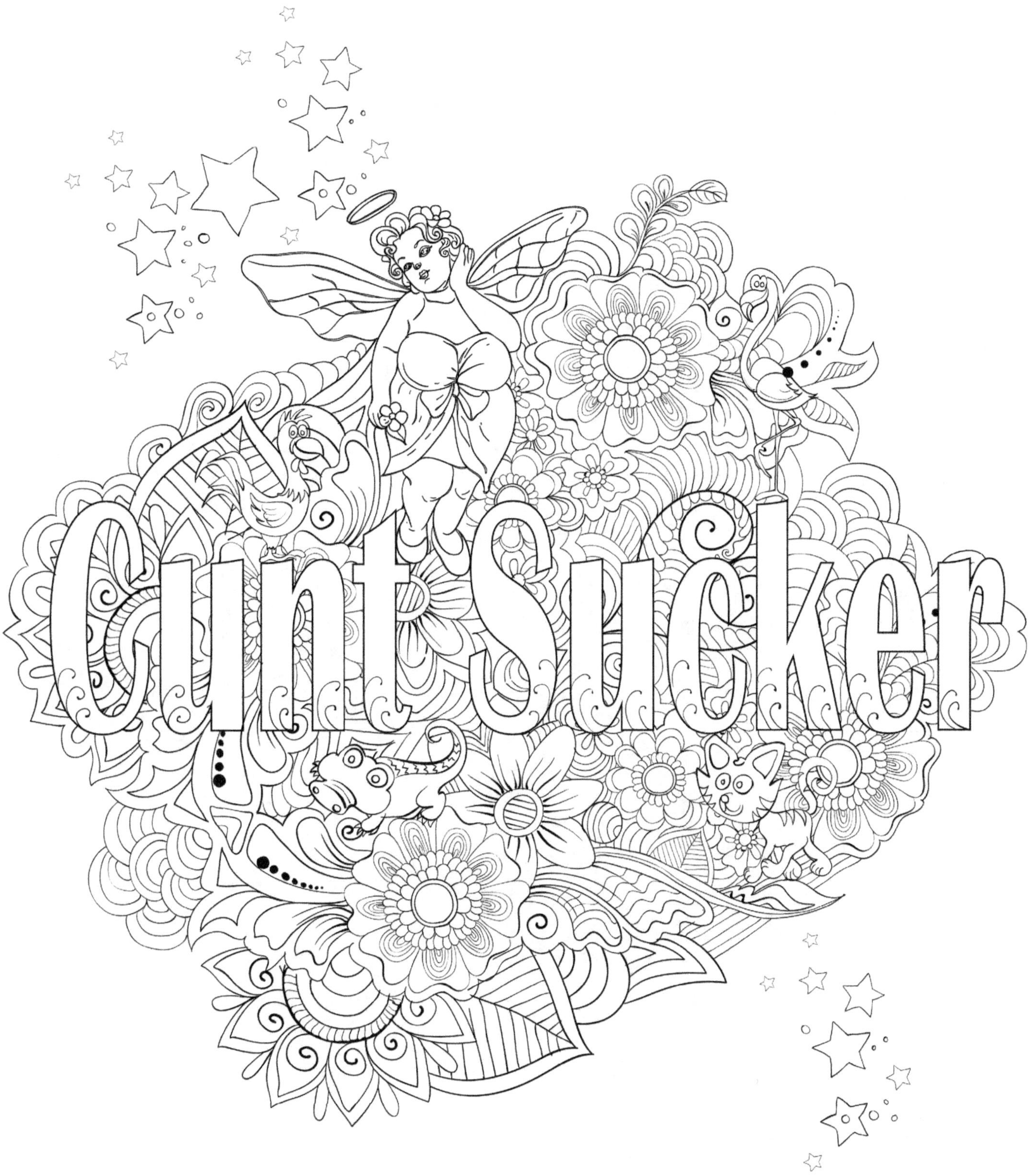
Cunt Sucker

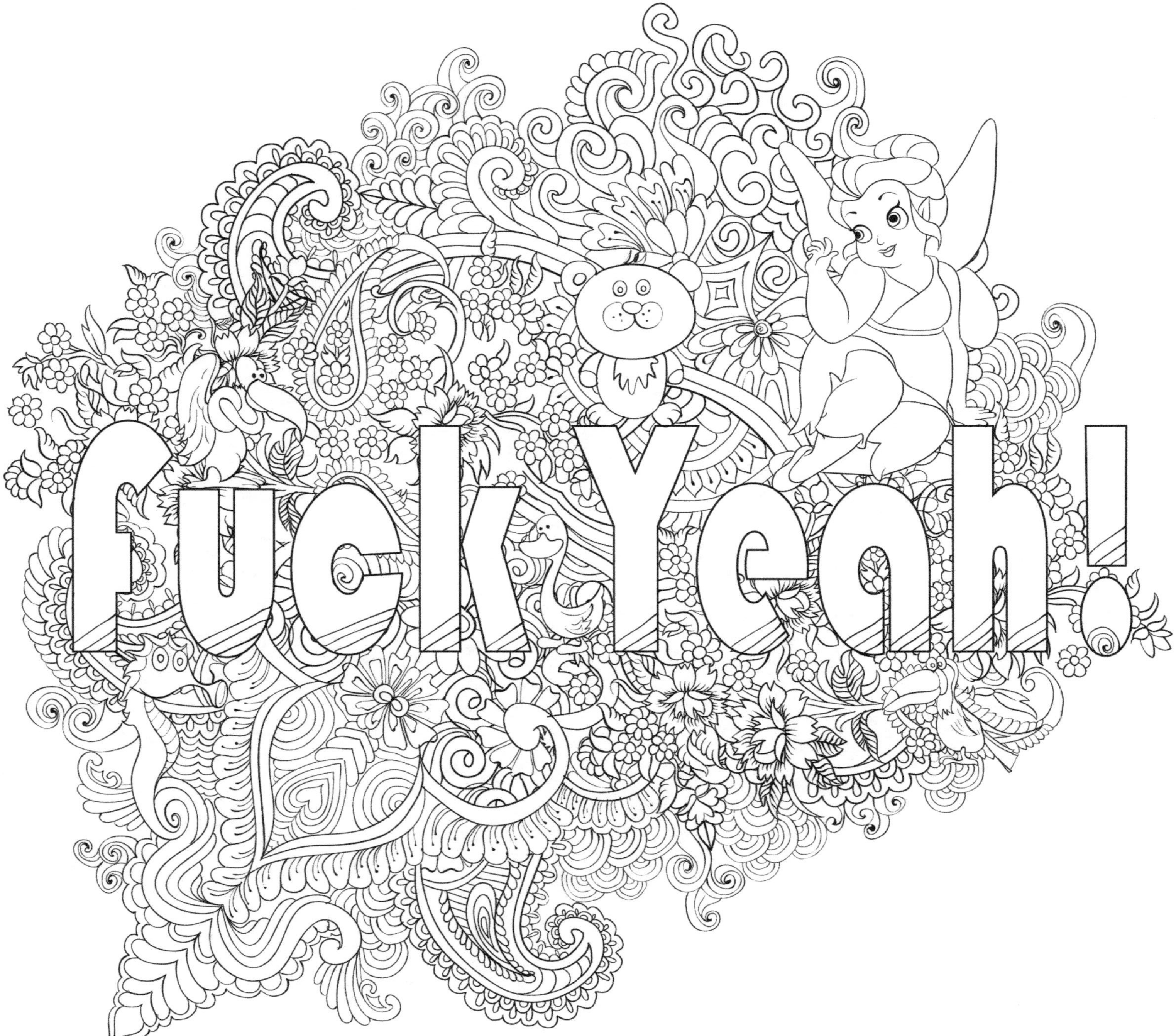
Fuck Yeah!

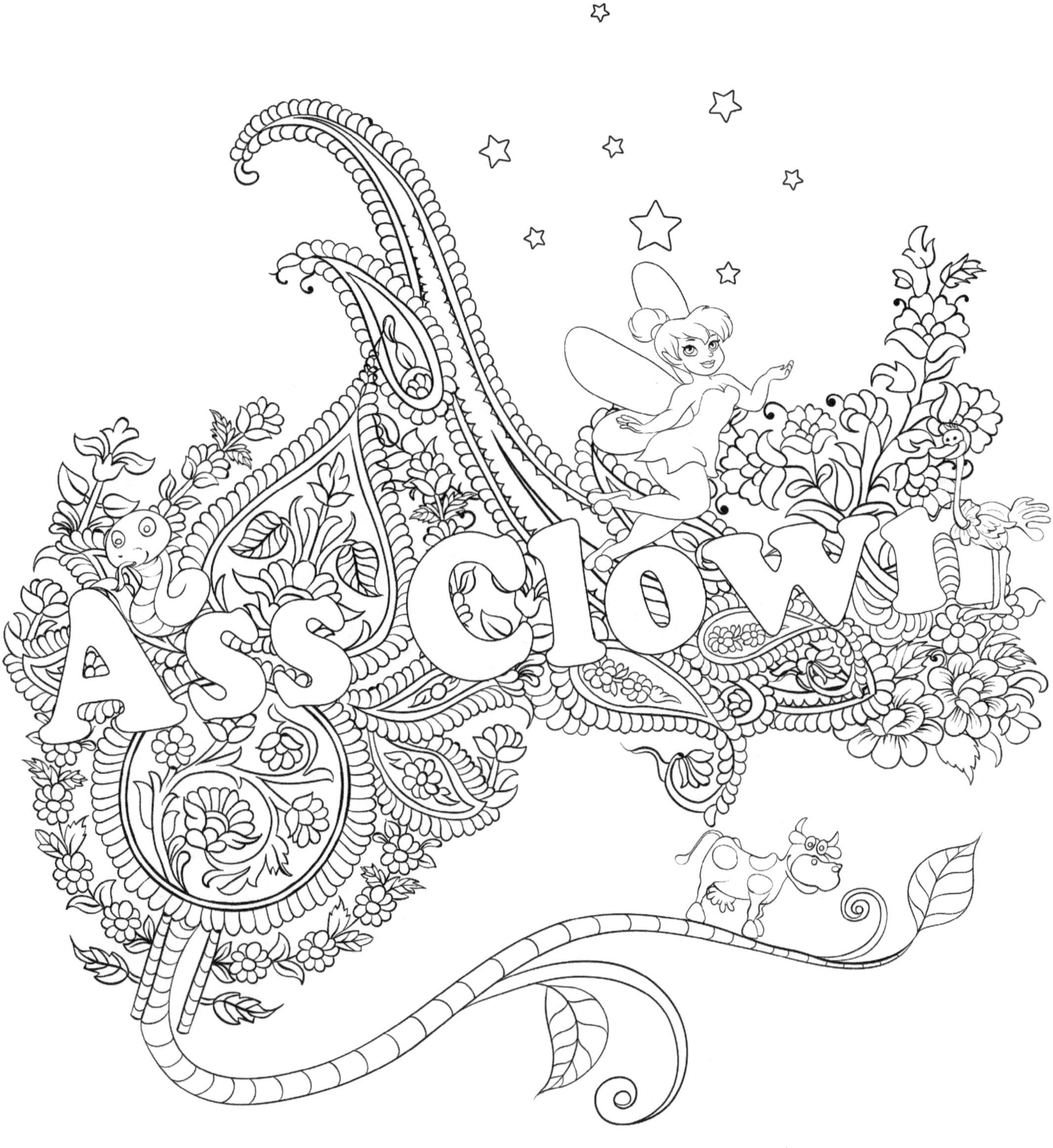
ASS Clown

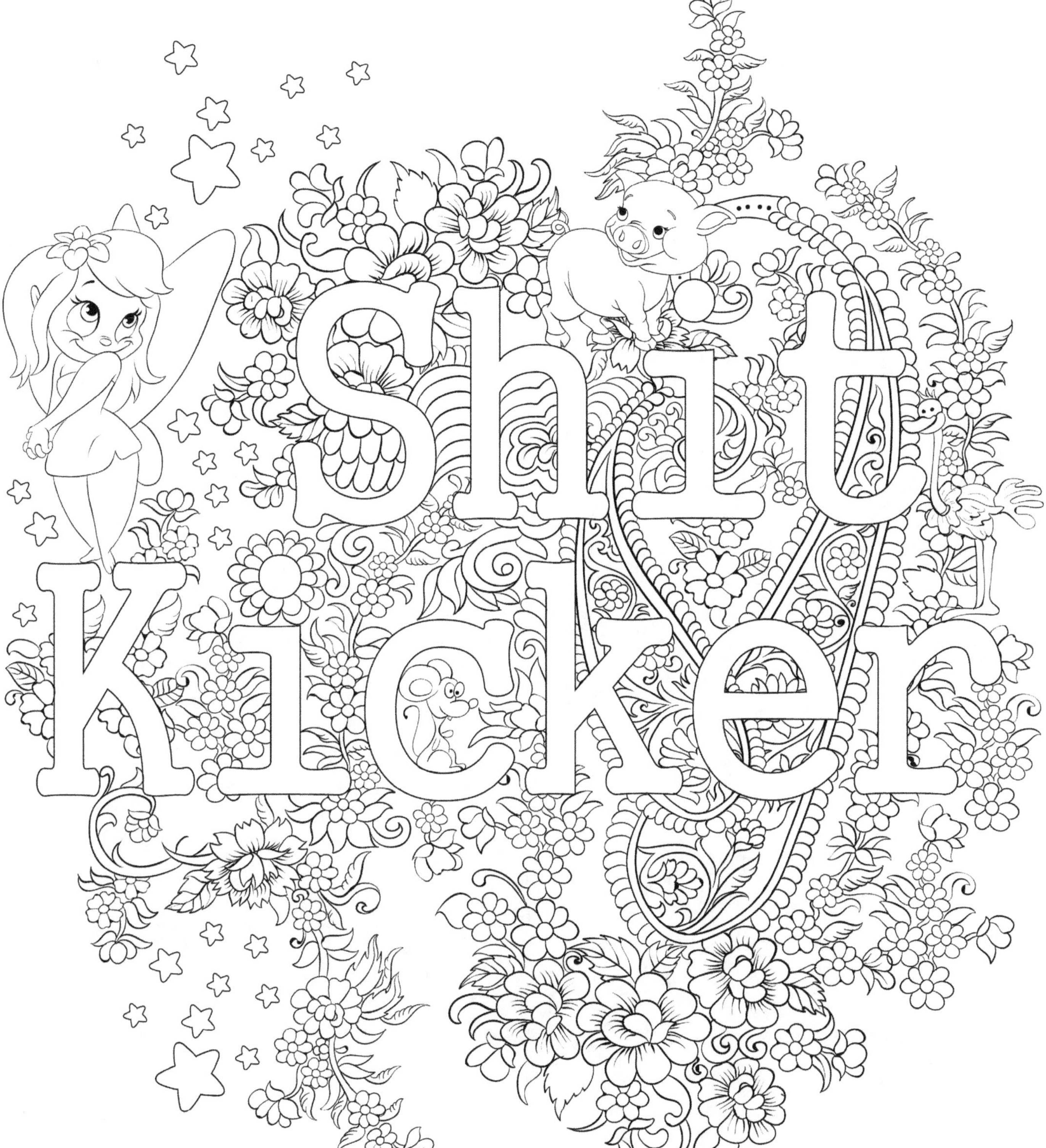
Shit
Kicker

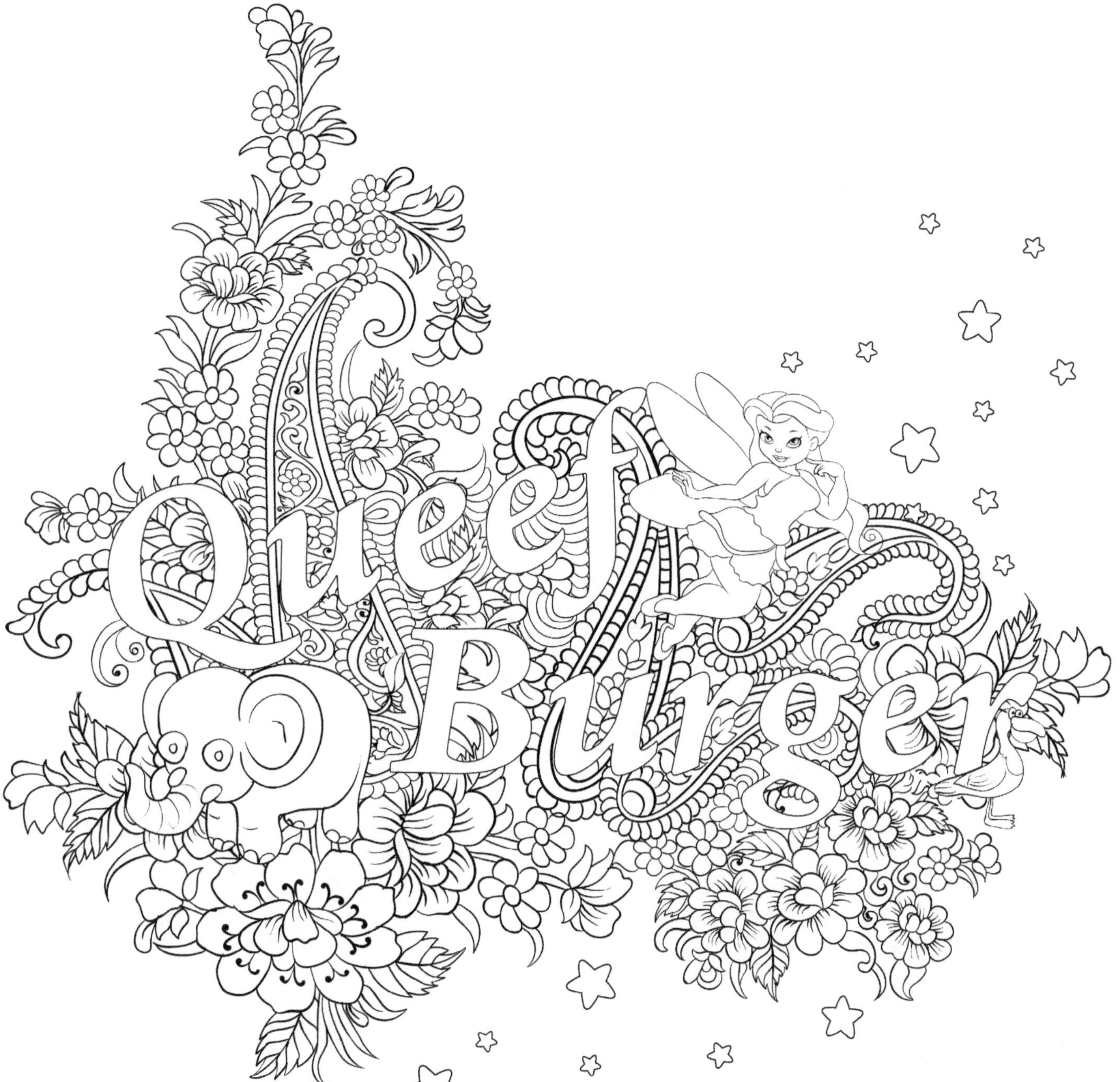
Queef
Burger

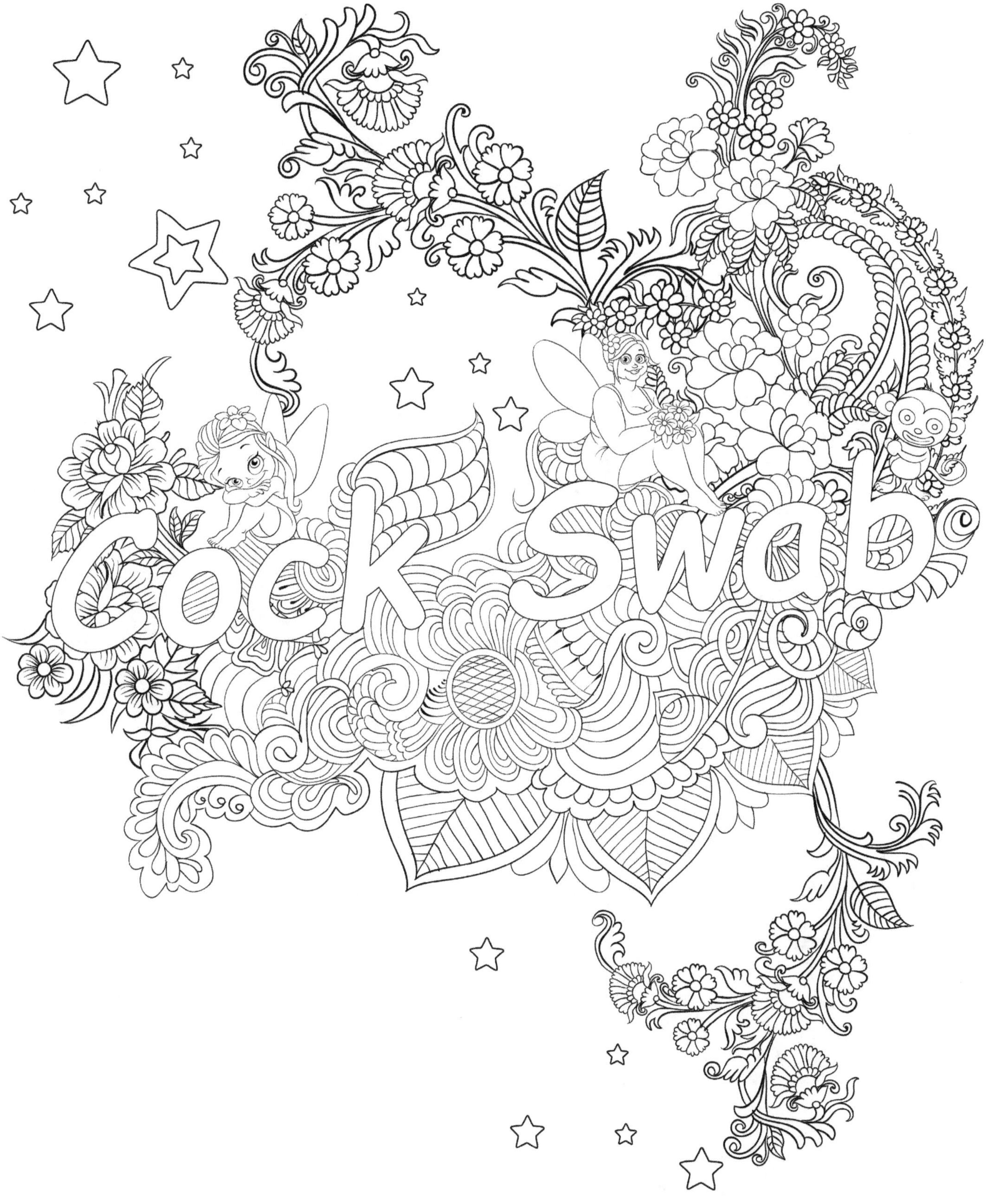
Cock Swab

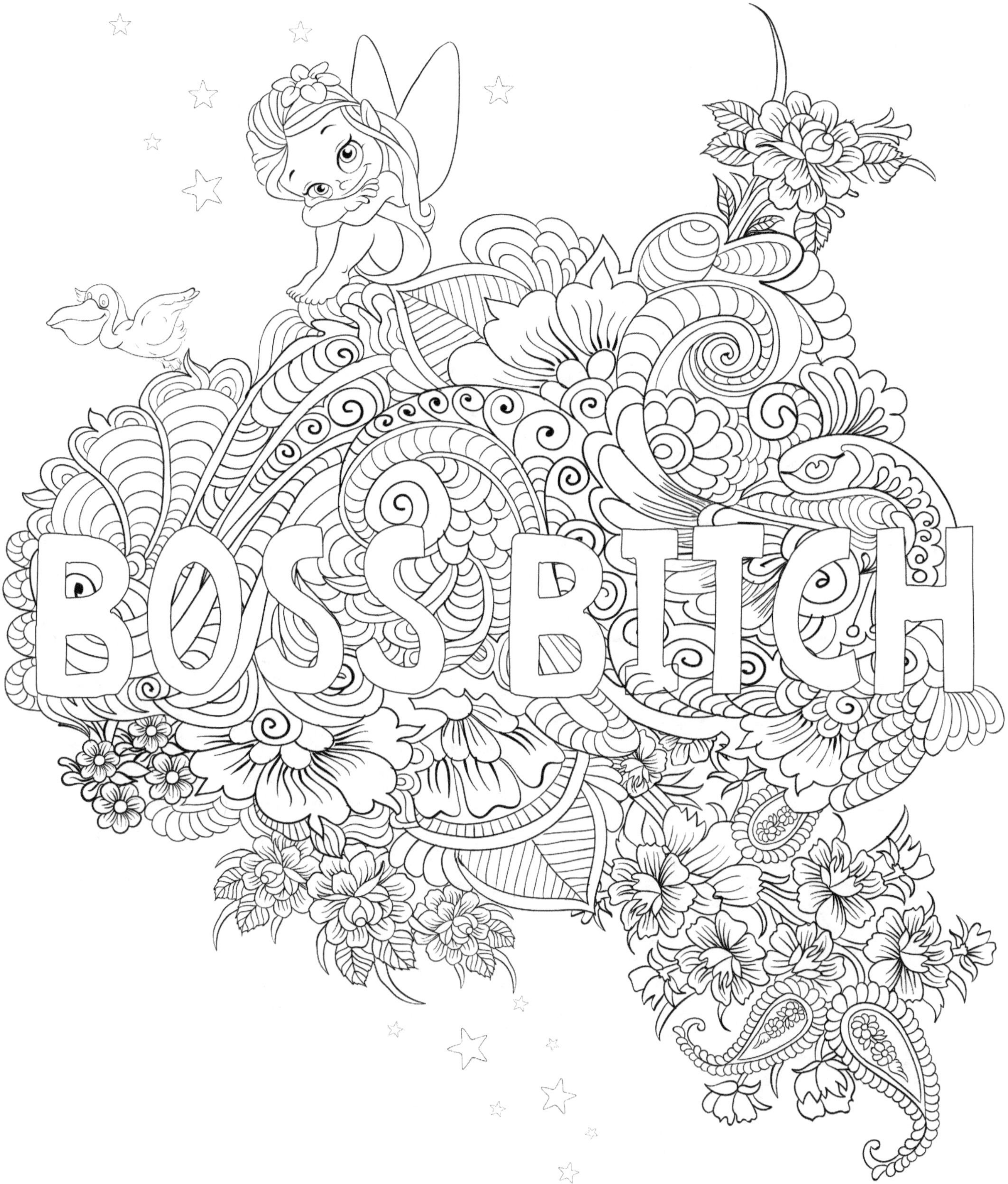
BOSS BITCH

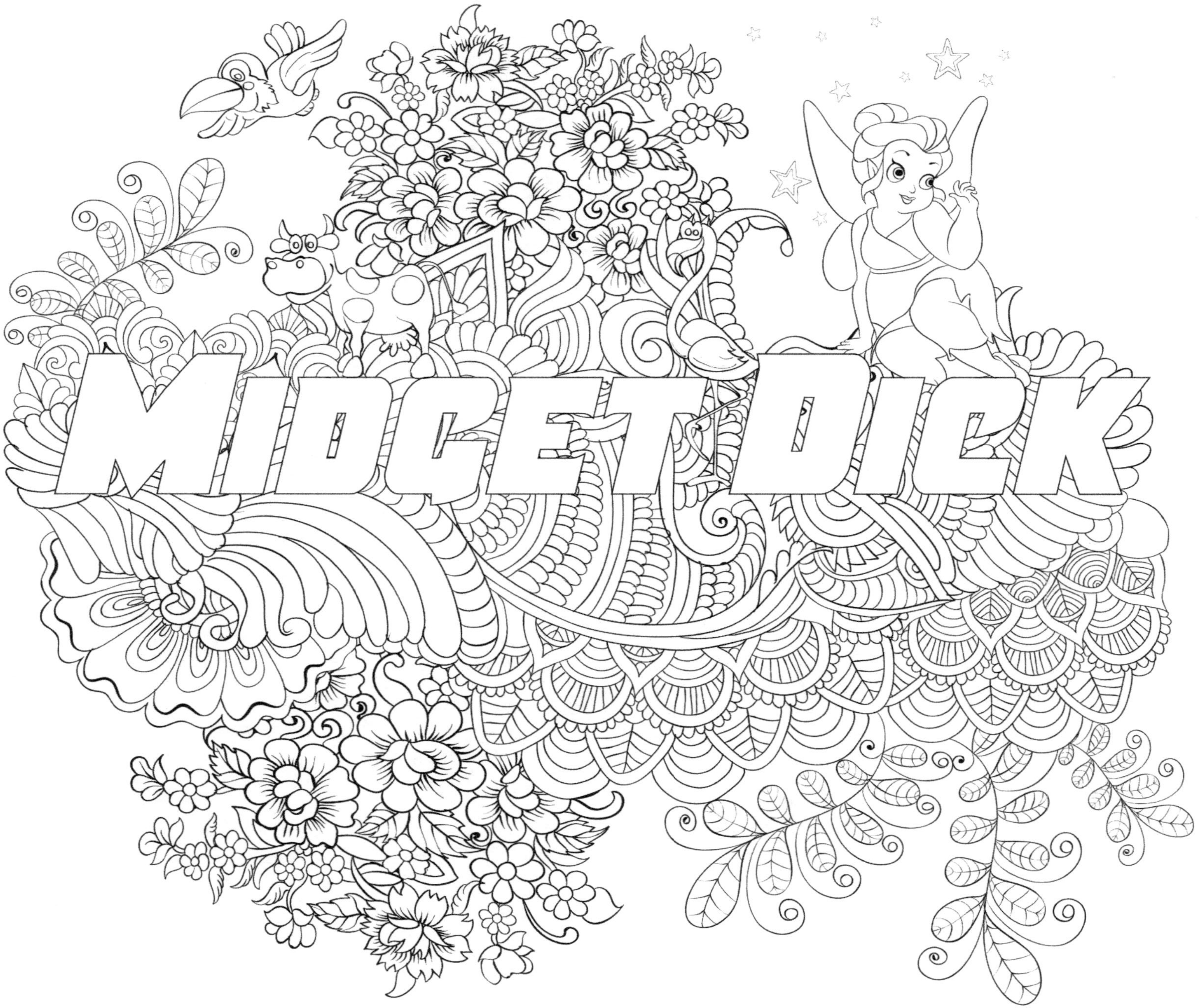
MIDGET DICK

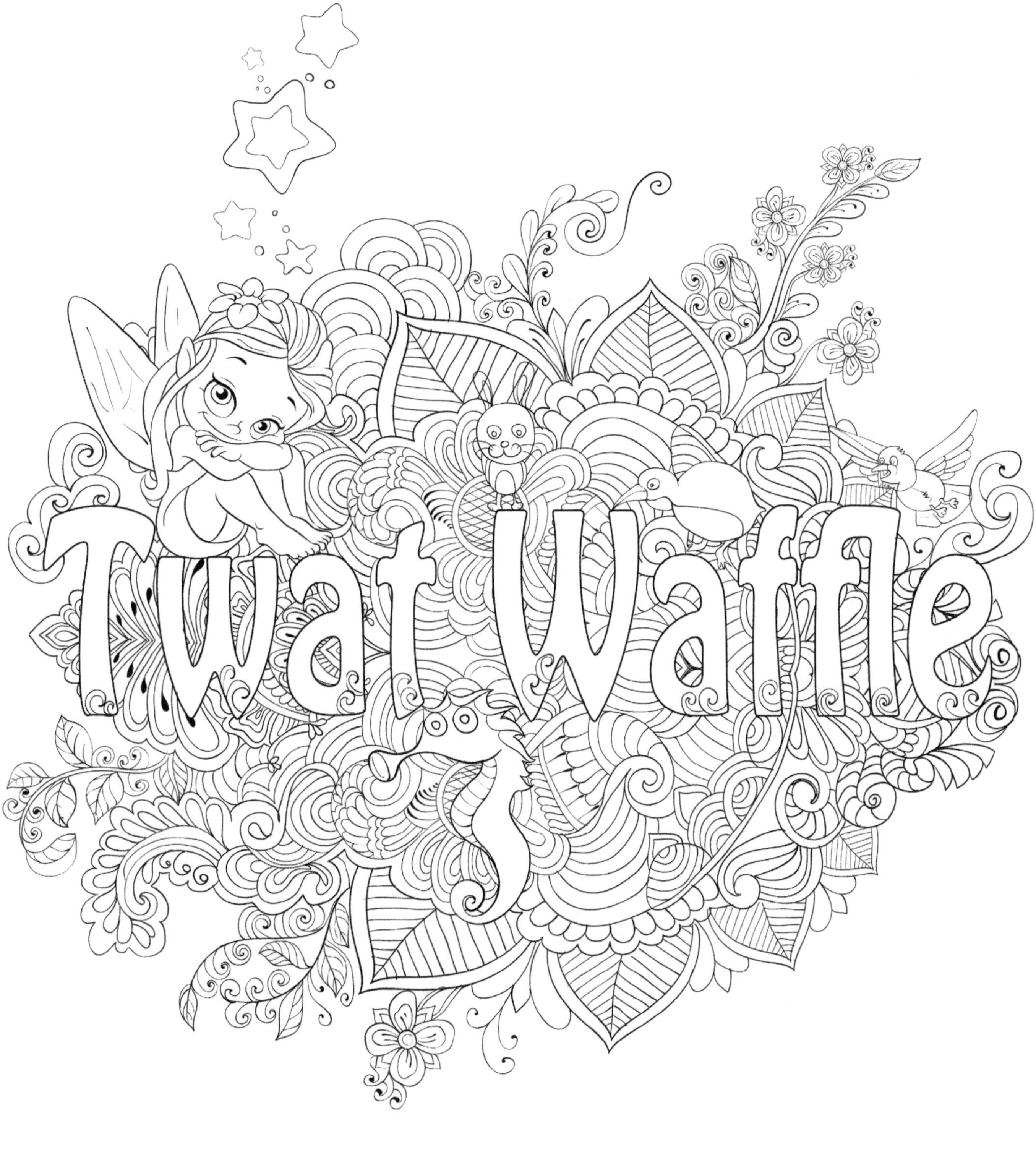
Twat Waffle

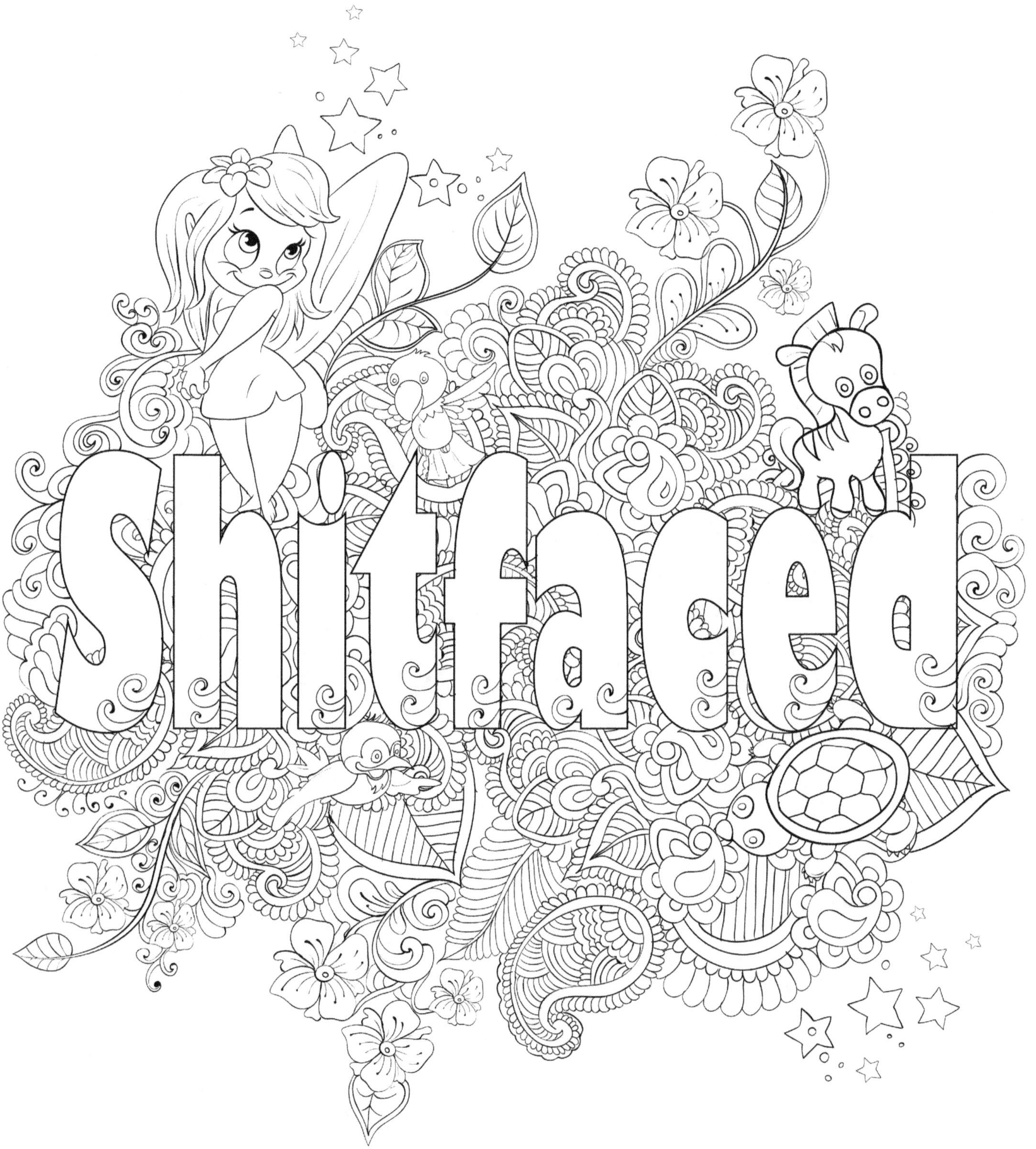
Shitfaced

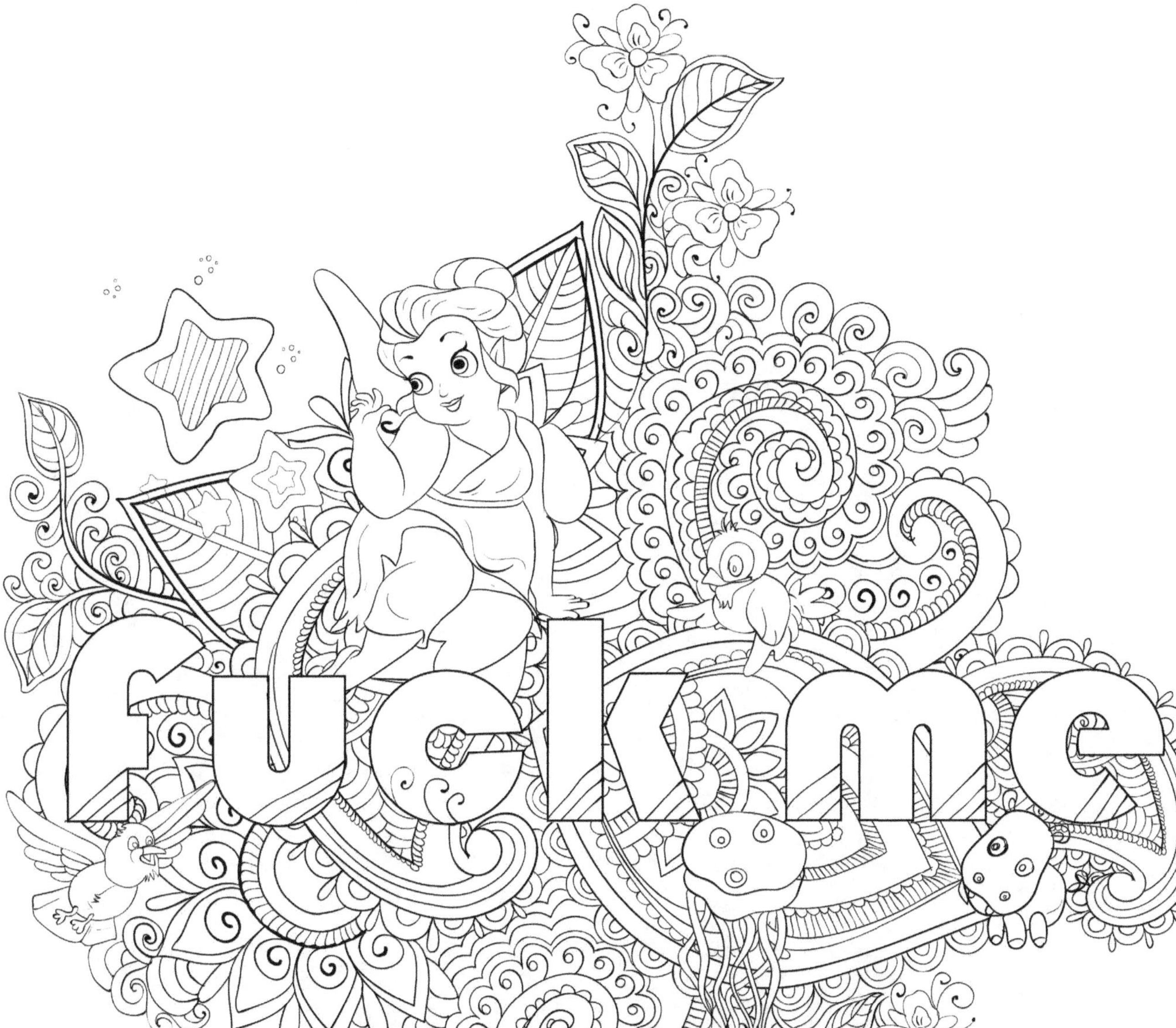
fuck me

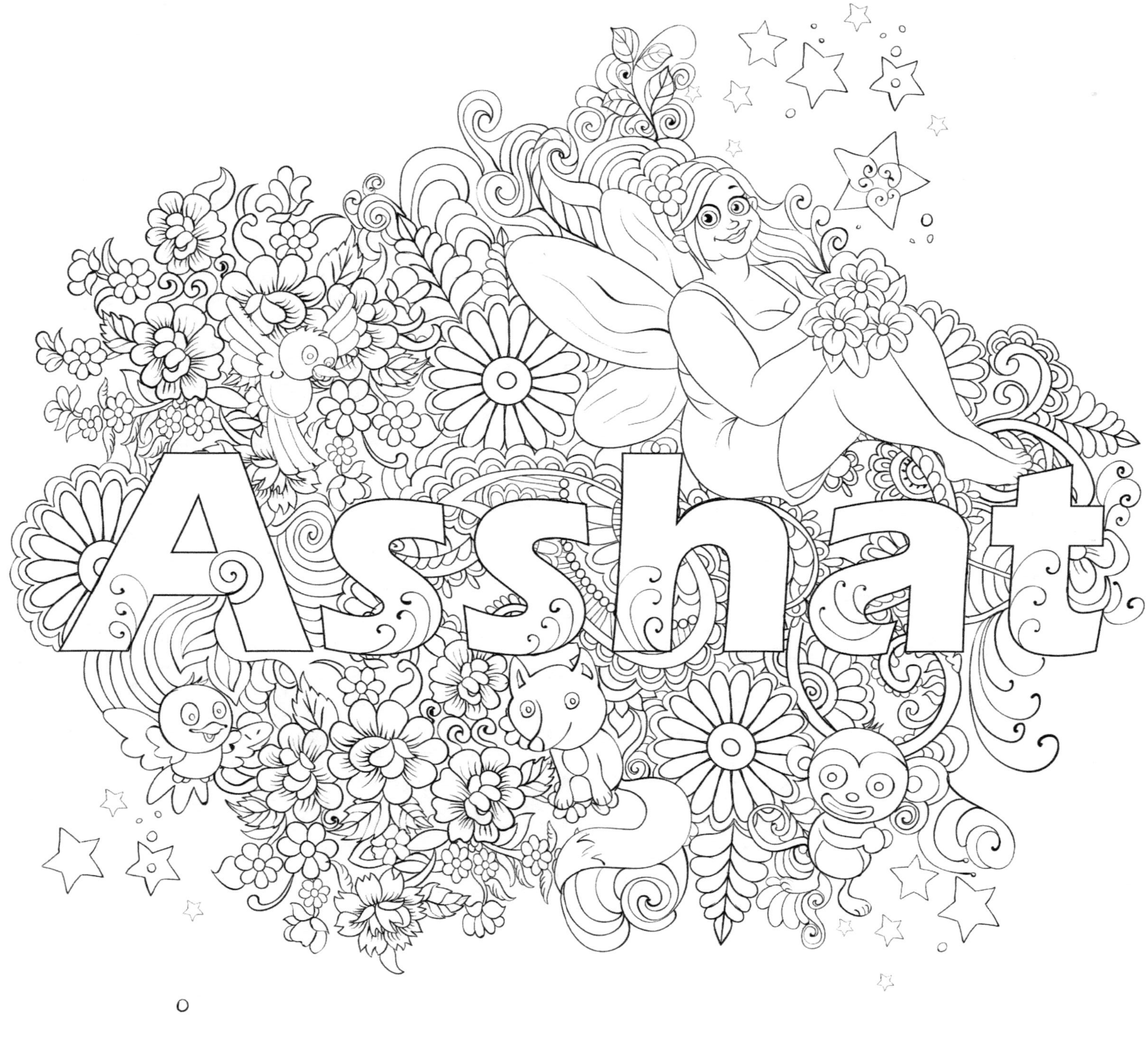
Asshat

www.ingramcontent.com/pod-product-compliance
Lightning Source LLC
Chambersburg PA
CBHW080636190526
45169CB00009B/3410
* 9 7 8 1 5 2 3 9 0 6 1 4 7 *